GETTING AROUND IN MY TOWN

TAKING A TRAIN

By Owen Hamlin

Consultant: Beth Gambro
Reading Specialist, Yorkville, Illinois

BEARPORT PUBLISHING

Minneapolis, Minnesota

Teaching Tips

Before Reading

- Look at the cover of the book. Discuss the picture and the title.
- Ask readers to brainstorm a list of what they already know about taking the train. What can they expect to see in the book?
- Go on a picture walk, looking through the pictures to discuss vocabulary and make predictions about the text.

During Reading

- Read for purpose. Encourage readers to think about the kinds of ways they can get around in their town.
- Ask readers to look for the details of the book. What are the steps to taking the train?
- If readers encounter an unknown word, ask them to look at the sounds in the word. Then, ask them to look at the rest of the page. Are there any clues to help them understand?

After Reading

- Encourage readers to pick a buddy and reread the book together.
- Ask readers to name two things they might do while taking the train. Find the pages that tell about these things.
- Ask readers to write or draw something they learned about taking the train.

Credits
Cover and title page, © Leonard Zhukovsky/Shutterstock; 3, © aapsky/Adobe Stock; 5, © Mlenny/iStock; 7T, © TJ Brown/Shutterstock; 7B, © EarthScapeImageGraphy/iStock; 8, © jorik/Shutterstock and © Ground Picture/Shutterstock; 9, © fizkes/iStock; 10–11, © carstenbrandt/iStock; 12, © NYC Stock Photos/iStock and © arum widyaningsih/Shutterstock; 13, © Ahmani Vidal/iStock; 14–15, © BeyondImages/iStock; 16–17, © carstenbrandt/iStock; 18–19, © Alex Segre/Shutterstock; 20, © Mdoculus/iStock; 21, © Imgorthand/iStock; 22, © gerenme/iStock, © pablorebo1984/iStock, and © Alex Gombash/iStock; 23TL, © Craig Russell/Shutterstock; 23TM, © Glynnis Jones/Shutterstock; 23TR, © Adrianocferreira/iStock; 23BL, © Elias Bitar/iStock; 23BR, © Lisa Marie/iStock.

See BearportPublishing.com for our statement on Generative AI Usage.

Library of Congress Cataloging-in-Publication Data

Names: Hamlin, Owen, 2000- author.
Title: Taking a train / by Owen Hamlin.
Description: Minneapolis, Minnesota : Bearport Publishing Company, [2025] |
Series: Getting around in my town | Includes bibliographical references
and index.
Identifiers: LCCN 2024025029 (print) | LCCN 2024025030 (ebook) | ISBN
9798892326308 (library binding) | ISBN 9798892327107 (paperback) | ISBN
9798892326704 (ebook)
Subjects: LCSH: Railroad trains--Juvenile literature. | Railroads--Juvenile
literature. | CYAC: Railroad trains. | Railroads.
Classification: LCC TF148 .H32127 2025 (print) | LCC TF148 (ebook) | DDC
625.2--dc23/eng/20240705
LC record available at https://lccn.loc.gov/2024025029
LC ebook record available at https://lccn.loc.gov/2024025030

For more information, write to Bearport Publishing, 5357 Penn Avenue South, Minneapolis, MN 55419.

Contents

All Aboard!

Today, we are going to the park.

It is far away.

How will we get there?

Let's take a train!

Loop

There are many kinds of trains.

Some go **underground**.

Others zoom along up high.

BLUE

Trains in our town go to different places.

Which one can get us where we need to go?

We look at a map on our phone to see.

We find the train we need.

The map also shows where the train stops.

We can get on at any of these train **stations**.

Say stations like STAY-shuhnz

At the station, we swipe our train **pass**.

This pays for the trip.

Beep!

A gate opens to let us in.

We go to the **tracks** for our train.

Many trains stop here.

Each one has a **sign**.

The signs say where the trains are going.

Say sign like SINE

Look, it is our train!

First, we stand back to let people get off.

Then, we get on.

Manhattan
& Brooklyn
N
To 86 St, Brooklyn via Manhattan Br.
Weekdays express, weekends local.
Late nights local via Lower Manhattan
W
Local to Whitehall St. Late
nights take N. Weekends
take N to Lex Av-59 St for R

Whoosh!

The train is fast.

Hold on!

We can sit down for the ride.

Or we can stand.

Standard

A map in the train tells us where we are.

We check it at every stop.

Finally, we get to the park.

I love taking the train!

Parts of a Train

A train gets us around our town. Let's look at its parts.

Glossary

pass a card or paper that is used to pay for things

sign a display that shows or tells something

stations places where trains stop

tracks a set of rails for a train to run on

underground below the ground level

Index

Read More

Golkar, Golriz. *Eco-Trains (Green Machines).* Minneapolis: Bearport Publishing Company, 2023.

Schuh, Mari. *Trains (Mega Machines).* Minneapolis: Kaleidoscope, 2022.

Learn More Online

1. Go to **FactSurfer.com** or scan the QR code below.
2. Enter "**Taking a Train**" into the search box.
3. Click on the cover of this book to see a list of websites.

About the Author

Owen has been on lots of trains! His favorite so far is the Tube in London, England.